Sparkling
Cocktails

Sparkling
Cocktails

More than 50 irresistible recipes
for fabulous fizz

LAURA GLADWIN

Photography by **ALEX LUCK**

An exclusive edition for

ALLSORTED.
for all your gift books and gift stationery

Watford, Herts, U.K. WD19 4BG

Dedication
For Emma

Senior Designer Toni Kay
Editorial Director Julia Charles
Production Controller Mai-Ling Collyer
Art Director Leslie Harrington
Publisher Cindy Richards

Drinks Stylist Tara Garnell
Prop Stylist Luis Peral
Indexer Hilary Bird

First published in 2018 by
Ryland Peters & Small
20–21 Jockey's Fields
London WC1R 4BW
www.rylandpeters.com

An exclusive edition for
Allsorted, Watford, Herts, U.K.
WD19 4BG

Recipe collection compiled by Laura
Gladwin and Julia Charles. Some of the
recipes in this book were first published
in Prosecco Cocktails (2017) and Parisian
Cocktails (2016), both by Laura Gladwin.

10 9 8 7 6 5 4 3 2 1

ISBN: 978-1-91229-540-1

A CIP record for this book is available from the
British Library. US Library of Congress CIP data
has been applied for.

Printed in China

Author's Acknowledgements
With thanks, as ever, to Niall Kishtainy.

Photography credits
All photography by Alex Luck with the
following exceptions:

Pages 4, 38 and 44 Kate Whitaker
Page 25 Mowie Kay

Contents

Introduction

Something cold and sparkling in an elegant glass – what a treat! Doesn't everyone enjoy a bit of bubbly at a wedding or birthday party, al fresco in the garden in summer, perhaps at a delightfully decadent breakfast or brunch? Now let's take those bubbles to a whole new level with easy-to-make sparkling cocktails for any occasion that your guests will love. There are recipes for sophisticated afternoon teas on the lawn, aperitifs that will add an extra touch of glamour to your next soirée and luxurious nightcaps to enjoy with that special someone.

Sparkling wine doesn't just mean the old favourites of Champagne and Prosecco: there's also Cava from Spain and Asti Spumante from Italy; various other French sparklers such as crémant de Loire, crémant de Limoux and crémant de Bourgogne; and Sekt from Germany. In fact, pretty much every wine-producing country, from England to Australia, makes their own fizz, catering for a range of budgets and flavour profiles.

Sparkling wine gets its bubbles through slightly different methods. Prosecco and Asti are made in a single fermentation in a large tank, after which the fizzy wine is bottled. These wines tend to have a fresh, fruity flavour, which has helped make them so popular in recent years. Champagne

bubbles come from a second stage of fermentation that takes place in the bottle, and Cava and the crémants are also made using this méthode traditionelle. This gives these wines the richer, toastier, more complex flavours so loved by the connoisseurs. However they're made, most sparkling wines are available in different levels of sweetness to suit every palate from brut or sec (dry), demi-sec (semi dry) to doux (sweet). Champagne, Prosecco and Cava are usually dry, though.

When it comes to making cocktails, there's no need to worry too much about the exact type of wine. Most of the drinks in this book will taste fabulous whatever type you use. Any dry sparkler can be used in place of another dry type, and the same goes for sweet varieties.

Cocktails do need to be properly cold, so make sure to chill your sparkling wine thoroughly before using it, and don't keep it hanging around once you've poured it out. If you're making cocktails for a party, scale up the recipes and mix the base ingredients in advance; then you can chill the mixture, pour a little in each glass and top up with the sparkling wine at the last minute.

You don't need much to get mixing: just a cocktail shaker, some ice and a few nice glasses. Whether it's a special occasion or just for the fun of it, a sparkling cocktail is always a delight!

Brunch Cocktails

Sanguinello Fizz

This sophisticated sparkler celebrates all the sweet, tart and bitter qualities of blood oranges, and will transport you to a fragrant Sicilian orange grove in no time.

40 ml/1$\frac{3}{4}$ oz blood orange juice

5 ml/1 teaspoon Campari

10 ml/$\frac{1}{3}$ oz limoncello

**well-chilled Prosecco or other dry sparkling wine,
to top**

blood orange wheel, to garnish

MAKES 1

Pour the first three ingredients into an ice-filled cocktail shaker and shake well. Strain into a chilled Champagne flute and top with Prosecco. Garnish with a blood orange wheel and serve.

Mango Morning

This is a bright, tropical sunshine-filled alternative to the classic Mimosa or Buck's Fizz. You won't be able to help being in a good mood if you're handed one of these.

15 ml/$\frac{1}{2}$ oz gin

50 ml/2 oz mango juice

5 ml/1 teaspoon freshly squeezed lemon juice

well-chilled Cava or other dry sparkling wine, to top

lemon zest twist, to garnish (optional)

MAKES 1

Pour the gin, mango juice and lemon juice into an ice-filled cocktail shaker and shake well. Strain into a chilled Champagne flute and top with Cava. Garnish with lemon zest, if you like, and serve.

Cranberry Cassis

This slightly dryer and fruitier twist on a Kir Royale would be perfect for a festive brunch gathering. The cranberry adds a little special Christmas magic, but it's refreshing and light at any time of year.

35 ml/1½ oz cranberry juice

15 ml/½ oz crème de cassis

well-chilled Prosecco or other dry sparkling wine, to top

redcurrants, to garnish (optional)

MAKES 1

Pour the first two ingredients into an ice-filled cocktail shaker and shake well. Strain into a chilled Champagne flute or small wine glass and top with Prosecco. Garnish with redcurrants, if you like, and serve.

Mimosa

Presenting the Bucks Fizz's chic cousin from across the pond: the Mimosa, which is beautifully enhanced by a dash of Cointreau.

about 65 ml/2¾ oz well-chilled freshly squeezed orange juice

5 ml/1 teaspoon Cointreau

about 65 ml/2¾ oz well-chilled Prosecco or other dry sparkling wine

MAKES 1

Half-fill a cold Champagne flute with the orange juice. Add the Cointreau and half the Prosecco. Stir gently, then add the rest and serve.

NOTE: If you're making a trayful, help the bubbles stay perky by adding half the Prosecco and stirring all the glasses. Finish off with the final dose of Prosecco just before serving.

Prosecco Mary

I like to think of the Prosecco Mary as the Bloody Mary's younger and slightly more glamorous sister. Why not ring the changes and wow your guests by serving these at your next brunch party?

25 ml/1 oz vodka

75 ml/3 oz tomato juice

dash of Tabasco or Sriracha sauce

pinch of sugar

dash of smoked water (optional, see note below)

about 75 ml/3 oz Cava or other dry sparkling wine

cucumber slices and/or a celery stick, to garnish

MAKES 1

Put the vodka, tomato juice, Tabasco, sugar and smoked water, if using, into a cocktail shaker half-filled with ice cubes. Shake vigorously and pour, ice cubes and all, into a chilled collins glass.

Add half the Prosecco and stir gently to combine. Top with the rest of the Prosecco, add some cucumber slices down the side of the glass (or a celery stick if you prefer) and serve with a paper straw and stirrer.

NOTE: Smoked water is fun and delicious but can overpower, so do exercise caution and use no more than 1/4 teaspoon to begin with. It is available in some larger supermarkets or to order from specialist online retailers.

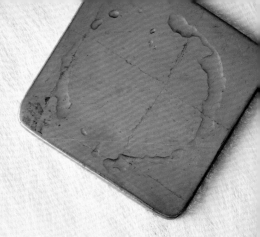

La Passeggiata

The passeggiata is an excellent Italian tradition of taking an evening stroll along a scenic boulevard, dressed up to the nines, to check out your neighbours. Why not give it a try down your road after breakfast, accompanied by one of these?

75 ml/3 oz chilled pink grapefruit juice
20 ml/⅗ oz gin
20 ml/⅗ oz Aperol
well-chilled Prosecco or other dry sparkling wine, to top
strip of grapefruit zest, to garnish (optional)
MAKES 1

Half-fill a collins glass with ice cubes. Add the pink grapefruit juice, gin and Aperol and stir well. Top with Prosecco and stir very briefly. If you like, squeeze a strip of grapefruit zest over the top and drop it in, then serve.

Jasmine Blossom

The beautiful floral perfume of jasmine tea, given a little backbone by a dash of gin and the almond scent of orgeat, makes this an unusual but delightful daytime cocktail that will intrigue your guests.

35 ml/1½ oz freshly brewed strong jasmine tea, chilled

5 ml/1 teaspoon orgeat syrup

10 ml/⅓ oz gin

well-chilled Asti Spumante or other semi-sweet sparkling wine, to top

jasmine leaves or blossoms, to garnish (optional)

MAKES 1

Pour the jasmine tea, orgeat syrup and gin into an ice-filled cocktail shaker and shake well. Strain into a chilled Champagne flute or small coupe and top with Asti. Garnish with jasmine, if you like, and serve.

Breakfast in Milan

Try one of these deliciously fruity and refreshing concoctions with a melt-in-the-mouth Italian pastry. Breakfast in bed, anyone?

3 teaspoons shredless orange marmalade

15 ml/½ oz freshly squeezed lime juice

dash of Campari (optional)

25 ml/1 oz gin

well-chilled Prosecco or other dry sparkling wine, to top

MAKES 1

Put the marmalade in a cocktail shaker with the lime juice, Campari, if using, and gin. Half-fill the shaker with ice cubes and shake vigorously. Strain into a cold martini glass, top with Prosecco and serve.

Elegant
Aperitifs

Sparkling Manhattan

If you love Manhattans but sometimes find them a bit much, you'll love this. This is based on a Sweet Manhattan, but feel free to switch the sweet vermouth for dry if you prefer yours dry – or use half sweet and half dry vermouth if you're more of a Perfect Manhattan fan.

15 ml/¹/₂ oz bourbon
10 ml/¹/₃ oz sweet red vermouth
dash of Angostura bitters
5 ml/1 teaspoon Maraschino, such as Luxardo (optional)
well-chilled Champagne or other dry sparkling wine, to top
maraschino cherries, to garnish

MAKES 1

Pour the first four ingredients into an ice-filled cocktail shaker and stir well.
Strain into a chilled old-fashioned glass and top with Champagne.
Garnish with maraschino cherries.

Aviation Royale

Channel the 1920s Jazz Age with this sparkling variation on the classic Aviation. It's based on a sophisticated combination of gin and Maraschino, with a splash of crème de violette for its perfume.

25 ml/1 oz gin

10 ml/¹⁄₃ oz freshly squeezed lemon juice

1¹⁄₂ teaspoons Maraschino, such as Luxardo

dash of crème de violette

well-chilled Champagne or other dry sparkling wine, to top

maraschino cherry, to garnish

MAKES 1

Pour the first four ingredients into an ice-filled cocktail shaker and stir well. Strain into a chilled Champagne coupe and top with Champagne. Garnish with a maraschino cherry and serve.

Kir Reali

The French have their Kir Royale (Champagne with crème de cassis), and the Kir Reali is the Italian version. All together now: When the moon hits your eye like a big pizza pie, that's amore...

10 ml/¹⁄₃ oz crème de violette

125 ml/4¹⁄₂ oz well-chilled Prosecco or other dry sparkling wine

strip of lemon zest, to garnish

MAKES 1

Pour the crème de violette into a chilled Champagne flute and add the Prosecco. Squeeze the lemon zest in half lengthways over the drink so that the essential oils in the skin spritz over it, then drop it in and serve.

Classic Champagne Cocktail

This is THE original sparkling cocktail, which dates back to the mid nineteenth century. Cognac was the spirit of choice, but Grand Marnier adds a pleasant citrus note. For this one, only Champagne will do - you need those toasty, biscuity flavours.

1 brown sugar cube

several dashes of Angostura bitters

25 ml/1 oz cognac or Grand Marnier, or a mixture of the two

well-chilled Champagne, to top

MAKES 1

Coat the sugar cube with Angostura bitters and drop it into a chilled Champagne flute. Chill the cognac and/or Grand Marnier in a separate glass by stirring it gently with ice cubes, then strain it into the Champagne flute. Top with Champagne and serve.

The Metropolis

Perhaps inspired by the Parisian café classic Kir Royale, the Metropolis combines crémant with the same appealing berry flavours, but adds a kick of vodka to give it a steely edge.

25 ml/1 oz vodka

25 ml/1 oz crème de framboise

well-chilled crémant de Bourgogne or other dry sparkling wine, to top up

MAKES 1

Fill a cocktail shaker with ice cubes and add the vodka and crème de framboise. Shake well and strain into a chilled cocktail glass. Top with crémant and serve.

Saint-Germain

A delicious and sprightly summer sparkler, perfect for imaginatively transporting yourself to the Parisian cafés of Saint-Germain-des-Près where Jean-Paul Sartre and Simone de Beauvoir once held court.

50 ml/2 oz well-chilled crémant de Loire
or other dry sparkling wine

35 ml/1$\frac{1}{2}$ oz elderflower liqueur,
such as St-Germain

soda water, to top

lemon zest, to garnish

MAKES 1

Fill a collins glass or tall tumbler with ice cubes.
Add the crémant and elderflower liqueur
and top with soda water.

Stir gently and garnish with a long strip of lemon zest.
Serve immediately.

French 75

Unlikely as it sounds, this was named for the gun used by
the French in World War I. It was a popular choice at Harry's New
York Bar in Paris, so feel free, while you sip, to imagine yourself in the
company of Hemingway and the Fitzgeralds...

25 ml/1 oz gin

10 ml/¹/₃ oz freshly squeezed lemon juice

5 ml/1 teaspoon sugar syrup

**well-chilled Champagne or other
dry sparkling wine, to top**

lemon zest, to garnish

MAKES 1

Fill a cocktail shaker with ice cubes, add the gin, lemon juice and sugar syrup
and shake well. Strain into a chilled Champagne flute.

Top with Champagne and garnish with a long strip of lemon zest.
Serve immediately.

Florida Breeze

The tartness of pink grapefruit awakens the appetite perfectly here. What summer lunch with friends wouldn't benefit from a little Florida sparkle?

35 ml/1½ oz pink grapefruit juice
15 ml/½ oz sweet red vermouth
dash of sugar syrup
dash of Angostura bitters

well-chilled Cava or other dry sparkling wine, to top
grapefruit zest, to garnish (optional)

MAKES 1

Pour the first four ingredients into an ice-filled cocktail shaker and shake well. Strain into a chilled Champagne flute, top with Cava and serve.

St Clements Fizz

This zesty creation really does sing of oranges and lemons, and makes a fabulous aperitif that will happily lend its dose of citrus sunshine to any occasion.

10 ml/⅓ oz Cointreau
10 ml/⅓ oz limoncello
10 ml/⅓ oz Aperol
dash of orange bitters (optional)

well-chilled Prosecco or other dry sparkling wine, to top
lemon and orange zest, to garnish

MAKES 1

Pour the first four ingredients into an ice-filled cocktail shaker and stir well. Strain into a chilled Champagne flute and top with Prosecco. Garnish with orange and lemon zest twists and serve.

Sbagliato

No need to worry about your hand 'slipping' with the gin here – sbagliato means 'mistaken', and this is a rough-and-ready, but rather delicious sparkling version, of the chic Negroni cocktail.

25 ml/1 oz sweet red vermouth
25 ml/1 oz Campari

75 ml/3 oz well-chilled Prosecco
or other dry sparkling wine

MAKES 1

Fill an old-fashioned glass with ice and add the vermouth and Campari. Stir well. Add the Prosecco, stir very gently to preserve the bubbles and serve.

Tiziano

This gorgeous concoction would be just perfect to kick off an intimate meal à deux. Dubonnet's Rouge Aperitif wine has been a staple on the cocktail landscape since 1846, and rightly so!

10 red grapes
75 ml/3 oz Dubonnet

well-chilled Prosecco or other
dry sparkling wine, to top
strip of orange zest, to garnish

MAKES 1

Put nine of the grapes into a cocktail shaker and muddle them to crush and extract the juice. Add a handful of ice cubes and the Dubonnet and shake vigorously. Strain into an old-fashioned glass, add some ice and top with Prosecco. Squeeze the zest lengthways to spritz the essential oils in the skin over the drink. Garnish with it and the remaining grape on a cocktail stick and serve.

Stiletto

This is simple yet delicious, and just like its fashionable namesake,
adding one to your next soirée will definitely make a statement.

25 ml/1 oz Amaretto

15 ml/¹/₂ oz freshly squeezed lime juice

well-chilled Cava or or other dry sparkling wine, to top

lime slice, to garnish

MAKES 1

Put the Amaretto and lime juice in a cocktail shaker with a handful of ice
and shake well. Strain into a chilled Champagne coupe, add the Prosecco and
garnish with a thin slice of lime. Serve immediately.

Al Fresco Fizz

Peach Julep

In the nineteenth century, mint juleps were sometimes made with peach brandy, and this rich, fruity and minty sparkler takes its inspiration from them. Perfect for hot summer nights.

5 mint leaves

20 ml/^{3}/$_4$ oz bourbon

25 ml/1 oz peach juice

5 ml/1 teaspoon peach schnapps

well-chilled Champagne or other
dry sparkling wine, to top

peach slice, to garnish

MAKES 1

Muddle the mint leaves with the bourbon in a cocktail shaker. Add the peach juice and peach schnapps with a handful of ice and shake well.

Strain into a chilled Champagne coupe, garnish with a peach slice and serve.

Summer Garden

Basil works beautifully when muddled with cucumber to create a lovely, light drink that's perfect for summer garden parties.

4-cm/1½-inch piece of cucumber, plus extra to garnish

5 basil leaves

5 ml/1 teaspoon sugar syrup

5 ml/1 teaspoon freshly squeezed lemon juice

well-chilled Cava or other dry sparkling wine, to top

MAKES 1

Cut the cucumber into small chunks and place in a cocktail shaker with the basil and sugar syrup. Muddle well to release all the juice. Add ice, stir well and then strain into a chilled Champagne flute. Top with Cava, garnish with a long strip of cucumber and serve.

Strawberry Fields Forever

The classic flavours of the Great British outdoors, and a guaranteed hit on a balmy summer evening wherever you are. Add a splash of sugar syrup if you're using dry sparkling wine.

2 strawberries, plus extra to garnish

5 mint leaves (optional)

15 ml/½ oz crème de fraise de bois

dash of freshly squeezed lemon juice

well-chilled Asti Spumante or other semi-sweet sparkling wine, to top

MAKES 1

Halve the strawberries and place in a cocktail shaker with the mint, if using, and crème de fraise de bois. Muddle well to release all the juices. Add the lemon juice and a handful of ice cubes and shake well. Strain into a chilled Champagne flute and top with Asti Spumante. Garnish with thin strawberry slices, if you like, and serve.

Pimm's Deluxe

Once you've tried this you'll wonder why you haven't been adding Prosecco to Pimm's all your life – it's a knockout! It is wise though to keep in mind that it packs more of a punch than your regular Pimm's and lemonade!

50 ml/2 oz Pimm's No 1 Cup
dash of elderflower cordial
sliced strawberries, orange, lemon and cucumber
well-chilled Prosecco or other dry sparkling wine, to top
a sprig of mint
MAKES 1

Fill a collins glass with ice cubes and add the Pimm's, elderflower and sliced fruit. Stir well, then half-fill with Prosecco. Stir gently, then add the rest of the Prosecco. Lightly crush the mint sprig and drop it in the top. Serve.

NOTE: If serving lots of people, make a pitcher of this ahead of time, which helps extract more flavour from the fruit, adding the ice, Prosecco and mint just before serving. For a 2-litre/2-quart pitcher, use 750 ml/26 oz Prosecco, 400 ml/14 oz Pimm's and 50 ml/2 oz elderflower cordial.

The Perfect Spritz

This simple Italian cocktail is THE drink of summer. Aperol is similar to Campari but sweeter in taste and has a relatively low alcohol content, making it perfect for warm summer afternoons.

35 ml/1½ oz Aperol

75 ml/3 oz well-chilled Prosecco or other dry sparkling wine

soda water, to top

orange slice, to garnish

MAKES 1

Half-fill a large wine glass or collins glass with ice cubes.
Pour in the Aperol and half the Prosecco and stir gently.
Add the rest of the Prosecco, top with a splash
of soda and add the orange slice. Serve.

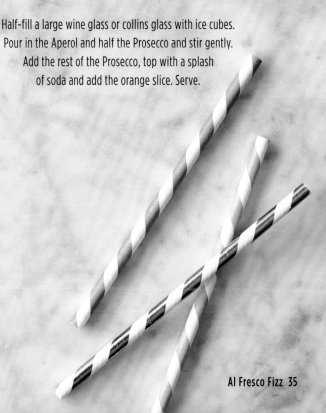

Seventh Heaven

Sweet vermouth and fresh mint provide the ideal backdrop for the tropical flavours in this chic and unusual cocktail that will keep your guests guessing... It's ambrosia for pineapple lovers.

5 mint leaves

5 ml/1 teaspoon sugar syrup

1 teaspoon freshly squeezed lemon juice

25 ml/1 oz pineapple juice

25 ml/1 oz sweet red vermouth

well-chilled Prosecco or other
dry sparkling wine, to top

pineapple wedge, to garnish (optional)

MAKES 1

Muddle the mint leaves, sugar syrup and lemon juice in a cocktail shaker. Add the pineapple juice and vermouth with a handful of ice cubes and shake well.

Strain into a chilled Champagne flute and top with Prosecco. Garnish with a long, thin wedge of pineapple, if you like, and serve.

Bellini

This famous cocktail was created in Harry's Bar, Venice in 1934. Mmmm, sitting on a palazzo terrace overlooking the Grand Canal, basking in the glow of the golden hour with an ice-cold Bellini in hand... it's the stuff of dreams...

35 ml/1½ oz good-quality, well-chilled peach juice or nectar

well-chilled Prosecco or other dry sparkling wine, to top

MAKES 1

Pour the peach juice into a cold Champagne flute. Half-fill with Prosecco and stir gently. Add the rest of the Prosecco and serve.

Rossini

Bring a little Italian culture to your get-together with this
stylish fizz that is named after the Italian opera composer
Gioachino Antonio Rossini.

15 ml/^{1}/$_2$ oz raspberry purée
5 ml/1 teaspoon Chambord
2 dashes of orange bitters
Champagne or other dry sparkling wine, to top up
MAKES 1

Add the purée, Chambord and bitters to a cold Champagne flute
and top up with Champagne. Stir gently and serve.

Viva España

Sangria with sparkling wine? Yes please! This is as refreshing as it is delicious. Switch the orange juice for blood orange or mandarin juice for delicious seasonal variations.

25 ml/1 oz Spanish red wine
15 ml/¹/₂ oz Dubonnet
25 ml/1 oz freshly squeezed orange juice
dash of sugar syrup

well-chilled Cava or other
dry sparkling wine, to top
orange slice, to garnish
MAKES 1

Pour the first four ingredients into an ice-filled cocktail shaker and shake well. Strain into a chilled Champagne flute or small wine glass and top with Cava. Garnish with an orange slice and serve.

Sangria Blanca

This peachy little number will get the fiesta started. Get out all your best cocktail 'furniture': this is no time to be tasteful.

¹/₄ ripe peach or nectarine, skin on
10 ml/¹/₃ oz freshly squeezed
lemon juice
25 ml/1 oz golden rum

15 ml/¹/₂ oz peach schnapps
25 ml/1 oz peach juice or nectar
well-chilled Prosecco, to top
MAKES 1

Thinly slice the peach and put it with the lemon juice, rum, peach schnapps and peach juice into a collins glass and stir well. Add a handful of ice cubes and top with Prosecco. Stir very gently, add your adornments and serve.

Party Sparklers

Havana Nights

In 1950s Havana, Ernest Hemingway used to drink his daiquiris at El Floridita and his mojitos at La Bodeguita. Now you can have the best of both worlds with this delicious sparkling version!

8 mint leaves

5 ml/1 teaspoon sugar syrup

10 ml/$^1/_3$ oz freshly squeezed lime juice

25 ml/1 oz aged (dark) rum

well-chilled Prosecco or
other dry sparkling wine, to top

lime zest or slice, to garnish (optional)

MAKES 1

Muddle the mint leaves with the sugar syrup in a cocktail shaker. Add the lime juice and rum with a handful of ice cubes and shake well. Strain into a chilled Champagne flute and top with Prosecco. Garnish with lime, if you like, and serve.

Tequila Slammer

Originally, the tequila slammer was a small glass of tequila topped with Champagne - you put your hand over the top and slam it down on the table to make the bubbles fizz up, then drink it quickly before it overflows. Here is a slightly more sophisicated take on the classic.

25 ml/1 oz tequila
15 ml/¹/₂ oz freshly squeezed lime juice
1 teaspoon sugar syrup

well-chilled Cava or other dry sparkling wine, to top
lime wedge, to garnish
MAKES 1

Pour the first three ingredients into an ice-filled cocktail shaker and shake well. Strain into a chilled old-fashioned glass and top with Cava. Garnish with a lime wedge and serve.

Jalisco Flower

Lovers of tequila will be wowed by this classy combination, which adds up to so much more than the sum of its parts.

15 ml/¹/₂ oz tequila
20 ml/³/₄ oz elderflower liqueur, such as St-Germain
35 ml/1¹/₂ oz pink grapefruit juice

well-chilled Cava or other dry sparkling wine, to top
edible flower, such as nasturtium or violet, to garnish
MAKES 1

Put the tequila, elderflower liqueur and pink grapefruit juice in a cocktail shaker and add a handful of ice cubes. Shake well and strain into a chilled martini glass. Top with Cava, garnish with an edible flower and serve.

Rosy Glow

Inspired by the classic cocktail Sex on the Beach, which was created in the 1980s – an era known for its provocatively named cocktails – this fruity concoction is dangerously drinkable!

10 ml/⅓ oz peach schnapps

10 ml/⅓ oz Chambord

15 ml/½ oz freshly squeezed orange juice

15 ml/½ oz cranberry juice

well-chilled Prosecco or other dry sparkling wine, to top

orange zest or fresh peach slice, to garnish

MAKES 1

Pour the first four ingredients into an ice-filled cocktail shaker and shake well. Strain into a chilled Champagne flute and top with Prosecco. Garnish with orange zest or a peach slice and serve.

Prosecco Cosmopolitan

You can bet that Carrie would have guzzled this in Sex and the City – THE classic girls'-night-out cocktail given extra sparkle!

25 ml/1 oz vodka

50 ml/2 oz cranberry juice

5 ml/1 teaspoon freshly squeezed lime juice

well-chilled Prosecco or other dry sparkling wine, to top

strip of orange zest, to garnish

MAKES 1

Put the vodka, cranberry juice and lime juice in a cocktail shaker with a handful of ice cubes. Shake well and strain into a chilled martini glass. Top with Prosecco. Squeeze the orange zest strip in half lengthways so that the essential oils in the skin spritz on to the drink, then drop it in and serve.

Cocomango

This delicous taste of the tropics is a lighter and more quaffable alternative to heavy coconut-based, tiki-style drinks.

15 ml/¹/₂ oz coconut rum, such as Malibu
15 ml/¹/₂ oz gin
25 ml/1 oz mango juice
10 ml/¹/₃ oz freshly squeezed lime juice

dash of Angostura bitters (optional)
well-chilled Asti Spumante or other semi-sweet sparkling wine, to top
dried mango strip, to garnish (optional)

MAKES 1

Pour the first five ingredients into an ice-filled cocktail shaker and shake well. Strain into a chilled Champagne flute and top with Asti Spumante. Garnish with a strip of dried mango, if you like, and serve.

Prosecco Passion

If you love the exotic taste of passion fruit, try this – a simplified sparkling twist on that absolute cocktail classic, the Porn Star.

25 ml/1 oz vodka
¹/₂ teaspoon vanilla paste or extract
1 teaspoon caster/superfine sugar
1 passion fruit

well-chilled Prosecco, to top
vanilla bean, to garnish (optional)

MAKES 1

Put the vodka, vanilla and sugar in a cocktail shaker. Halve the passion fruit, scoop out all the flesh and seeds and drop them in the shaker. Add a handful of ice cubes and shake vigorously. Strain into a chilled martini glass, top with Prosecco and serve, with a vanilla bean stirrer to garnish, if you like.

Hibiscus Fizz

Hibiscus flowers are said to have health benefits, but never mind all that, let's drown them in some fizz! Jars of these beautiful flowers preserved in syrup are widely available now, and add a lovely pink colour and sweet, fruity tang to your bubbles. It couldn't be easier.

1 wild hibiscus flower in syrup
dash of the hibiscus syrup or crème de framboise (optional)
well-chilled Asti Spumante or other
semi-sweet sparkling wine, to top
MAKES 1

Carefully place the hibiscus flower with the petals facing upwards in the bottom of a chilled Champagne flute. Add the hibiscus syrup or crème de framboise, if using. Slowly pour in the Asti Spumante and serve.

Cherry Baby

Bakewell tart in a glass, you say? Yes please! Lovers of cherry
and almond cake everywhere will be delighted with this.

25 ml/1 oz Amaretto
15 ml/$\frac{1}{2}$ oz kirsch or cherry brandy
25 ml/1 oz cherry juice
well-chilled Asti Spumante or other
semi-sweet sparkling wine, to top
MAKES 1

Put the Amaretto, kirsch and cherry juice in a cocktail shaker and add a handful
of ice cubes. Shake well, then strain into an old-fashioned glass, top with
Prosecco and serve.

Prima Donna

Let your inner diva enjoy this dazzling pomegranate
and limoncello number! Quite a performance.

25 ml/1 oz vodka
15 ml/$\frac{1}{2}$ oz limoncello
25 ml/1 oz pomegranate juice
well-chilled Prosecco, to top
MAKES 1

Put the vodka, limoncello and pomegranate juice in a cocktail shaker and add
a handful of ice cubes. Shake well and strain into a chilled Champagne flute,
top with Prosecco and serve.

Appleblack

The perfect choice for a sophisticated drinks party, the Appleblack offers a more potent alternative to the Kir Royale. Its apple and blackcurrant flavours make it ideal for autumn and winter gatherings.

15 ml/¹⁄₂ oz Calvados
15 ml/¹⁄₂ oz crème de cassis

well-chilled crémant de Loire or other dry sparkling wine, to top

MAKES 1

Pour the Calvados and crème de cassis into an ice-filled cocktail shaker and stir well. Strain into a chilled Champagne flute, top with crémant de Loire and serve.

Night Owl

Any night owl worth their salt, and even a few who should know better, will enjoy this wickedly drinkable creation.

15 ml/¹⁄₂ oz gin
15 ml/¹⁄₂ oz crème de cassis
15 ml/¹⁄₂ oz pomegranate juice

well-chilled Prosecco or other dry sparkling wine, to top
strip of lemon zest, to garnish

MAKES 1

Put the gin, cassis and pomegranate juice in a cocktail shaker with a handful of ice cubes and shake well. Strain into a chilled martini glass and top with Prosecco. Squeeze the lemon zest strip in half lengthways so that the essential oils in the skin spritz on to the drink, then drop it in and serve.

Romantic Sippers

Chocoholic

Not all chocolate drinks have to be sweet, rich and creamy. This one combines the rich taste of cocoa with the toasted hazelnut flavour of Frangelico to make the perfect sparkler for chocolate lovers. Anyone who enjoys their fizz and chocolate will be on to a winner.

finely crushed chocolate or cocoa powder,
to garnish (optional)

20 ml/³⁄₄ oz crème de cacao

10 ml/¹⁄₃ oz Frangelico

dash of lemon juice

well-chilled Asti Spumante or other
semi-sweet sparkling wine, to top

MAKES 1

If using the garnish, moisten the rim of a chilled Champagne coupe and dip it carefully into finely crushed chocolate or cocoa powder. Pour the crème de cacao, Frangelico and lemon juice into an ice-filled cocktail shaker and shake well. Strain carefully into the glass, top with Asti Spumante and serve.

Liaisons Dangereuses

This seductive combination of bourbon whiskey, orange liqueur and Amaretto, lifted with a luxurious spritz of Champagne, would make a decadent finale for a romantic meal.

15 ml/½ oz bourbon
10 ml/⅓ oz Cointreau
5 ml/1 teaspoon Amaretto

well-chilled Champagne or other dry sparkling wine, to top
orange zest twist, to garnish (optional)

MAKES 1

Pour the first three ingredients into an ice-filled cocktail shaker and stir well. Strain into a chilled Champagne coupe and top with Champagne. Garnish with orange zest, if you like, and serve.

The Impressionist

A wistfully romantic cocktail that may evoke feelings of nostalgia... Here the luscious scents of cherry, raspberry and violet recreate the joyous colours of French impressionist painter Monet's garden.

15 ml/½ oz Grand Marnier Cherry
15 ml/½ oz raspberry syrup
5 ml/1 teaspoon Parfait Amour violet liqueur

well-chilled Champagne or other dry sparkling wine, to top up

MAKES 1

Fill a cocktail shaker with ice cubes. Add the Grand Marnier cherry, raspberry syrup and Parfait Amour and shake well. Strain into a chilled cocktail glass, top up with Champagne and serve.

Babycakes

Look no further for the ultimate Valentine's cocktail. Berries and rosewater are dreamy together, and what could be more romantic than sipping a couple of these at sunset?

15 ml/½ oz vodka

10 ml/⅓ oz Chambord

10 ml/⅓ oz crème de fraise de bois or other strawberry liqueur

½ teaspoon rosewater

well-chilled Asti Spumante or other semi-sweet sparkling wine

edible rose petal or strawberry, to garnish (optional)

MAKES 1

Pour the first four ingredients into an ice-filled cocktail shaker and stir well. Strain into a chilled Champagne flute and top with Asti Spumante. Garnish with a rose petal or halved strawberry, if you like, and serve.

Rosebud

Feisty yet delicate, and strangely captivating... no, not a plucky romantic heroine, but a rather lovely little drink.

5 ml/1 teaspoon rosewater

20 ml/¾ oz elderflower liqueur, such as St-Germain

15 ml/½ oz gin

1 teaspoon freshly squeezed lemon juice

well-chilled Prosecco or other dry sparkling wine, to top

edible rose petal, to garnish (optional)

MAKES 1

Put the rosewater, elderflower liqueur, gin and lemon juice in a cocktail shaker. Add a handful of ice and shake well. Strain into a chilled Champagne flute and top with Prosecco. Garnish with arose petal and serve.

Lillet de Loire

Lillet is a perfumed aperitif wine made in Bordeaux, France.
Combined here with French dry sparkling wine and sharpened
with lemon juice, it makes the perfect start to any romantic evening.

50 ml/2 oz Lillet

1 teaspoon freshly squeezed
lemon juice

well-chilled crémant de Loire or other
dry sparkling wine, to top

MAKES 1

Pour the Lillet and lemon juice into an ice-filled cocktail shaker.
Stir well, strain into a chilled cocktail glass, top with crémant de Loire and serve.

Posy

Didn't receive any flowers on Valentine's Day? Fear not, blossomy
scents abound in this semi-dry and refined blend of floral flavours
so simply pep yourself up with a glass of this delicious concoction.

1 teaspoon crème de violette

10 ml/$\frac{1}{3}$ oz elderflower liqueur,
such as St-Germain

5–10 ml/1 teaspoon–$\frac{1}{3}$ oz grenadine,
to taste

dash of freshly squeezed lemon juice

well-chilled Crémant de Loire or other
dry sparkling wine, to top

edible flower, to garnish (optional)

MAKES 1

Pour the first four ingredients into an ice-filled cocktail shaker and stir well.
Strain into a chilled Champagne glass or small Collins glass and top with
Crémant de Loire. Garnish with an edible flower, if you like, and serve.

Bridge of Sighs

This was named after the famous enclosed bridge in Venice, under which, legend has it, lovers will be granted eternal bliss if they kiss on a gondola at sunset. Tempting though that sounds, it might be easier to simply drink one of these together, and sigh with bliss…

caster/superfine sugar,
to decorate the glass (optional)
15 ml/$\frac{1}{2}$ oz gin
15 ml/$\frac{1}{2}$ oz elderflower liqueur, such as St-Germain
well-chilled Prosecco or other dry sparkling wine, to top
MAKES 1

If you like, moisten the rim of a chilled Champagne flute with water and dip it into a saucer filled with caster/superfine sugar to create a rim around the glass. Put the gin and elderflower liqueur in a cocktail shaker with a handful of ice cubes and stir. Strain carefully into the flute.

Add half the Prosecco and stir gently, then add the rest and serve.

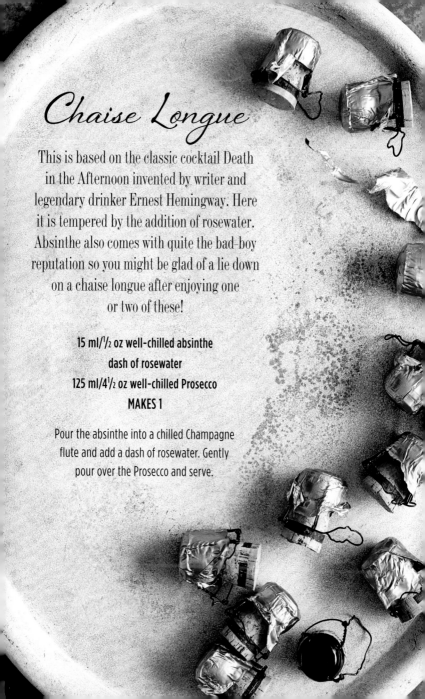

Chaise Longue

This is based on the classic cocktail Death in the Afternoon invented by writer and legendary drinker Ernest Hemingway. Here it is tempered by the addition of rosewater. Absinthe also comes with quite the bad-boy reputation so you might be glad of a lie down on a chaise longue after enjoying one or two of these!

15 ml/$\frac{1}{2}$ oz well-chilled absinthe
dash of rosewater
125 ml/$4\frac{1}{2}$ oz well-chilled Prosecco
MAKES 1

Pour the absinthe into a chilled Champagne flute and add a dash of rosewater. Gently pour over the Prosecco and serve.

Index